BRITAIN SINCE 1948

Population and Settlement

Peter Hepplewhite

WAYLAND

First published in 2008 by Wayland

Copyright © Wayland 2008

Wayland
338 Euston Road
London NW1 3BH

Wayland Australia
Level 17/207 Kent Street
Sydney, NSW 2000

Editor: Katie Powell
Designer: Peta Phipps
Illustrator: Peter Bull Art Studio

British Library Cataloguing in Publication Data

Hepplewhite, Peter
Population and settlement. - (Britain since 1948)
1. Human settlements - Great Britain - History - 20th century - Juvenile
literature
2. Social change - Great Britain - History - 20th century - Juvenile literature
3. Great Britain - Population - History - 20th century - Juvenile literature
4. Great Britain - Social conditions - 20th century - Juvenile literature
I. Title
307.1'4'0941'09045

ISBN 978 0 7502 5376 5

Printed in China

Wayland is a division of Hachette Children's Books, an Hachette Livre UK
company.

Picture acknowledgements: AP/Topham: 27, BBC/Corbis: 24,
Bettmann/Corbis: 20, Ann Biyajian/Illustration Works/Corbis: 13, Russell
Boyce/Reuters/Corbis: 25, Corbis: 22, Tim Graham/Corbis: front cover, 15,
Hulton-Deutsch/Corbis: 5, Edward G. Malindine/Hulton Archive/Getty Images:
6, Max Nash/AFP/Getty Images: 8, National Pictures/Topfoto: 21, OM/Topfoto:
10,11, petsforsberg/Alamy: 23, Picturepoint/Topham: front cover, 19.
Popperfoto: 12, Roger-Viollet/Topfoto: 4, Sipa/Rex Features: 9, Selwyn
Tait/Sygma/Corbis: 16, Harry Todd/Hulton Archive/Getty Images: 26.
Topfoto: 7, Wayland: 28.

Every effort has been made to clear copyright. Should there be any
inadvertent omission please apply to the publisher for rectification.

The website addresses (URLs) included in this book were valid at the
time of going to press. However, because of the nature of the Internet,
it is possible that some addresses may have changed, or sites may have
changed or closed down since publication. While the author and Publisher
regret any inconvenience this may cause the readers, no responsibility for
any such changes can be accepted by either the author or the Publisher.

Contents

Words in **bold** can be found in the glossary.

Britain in 1948

If you could go back in time and visit Britain in 1948 you might be disappointed by how grey and tired the country seemed. The cost of winning the Second World War in 1945 had been enormous – 388,000 military and civilian dead and more than a million injured. The nation had been saved from going broke by a huge loan of $4 billion from America in 1947.

Voices from history

'Let us pray, that by God's good grace the vast range of modern knowledge which is here shown may be turned from destructive to peaceful ends, so that all people, as the century goes on, may be lifted to greater happiness.'

King George VI, 3 May 1951, at the opening of the Festival of Britain.

Wartime Shortages Continue

To the growing anger of most people, wartime rationing not only continued, it got worse. The meat ration was at its smallest in 1951 and, to the dismay of children, sweet rationing didn't end until 1953. Most towns and cities still showed the raw scars of air raid damage and, because materials like wood and cement were in short supply, rebuilding had hardly begun. Industry and transport, especially the railways, were worn out by seven years of demanding wartime work. Investment in new buildings and equipment was badly needed.

TIMELINE

	1945	The end of the Second World War
	1948	160,000 emergency houses called prefabs built at a cost of £1,300 each
	1951	More than 2,000 towns and villages organise special events for the Festival of Britain and more than 18 million people take part
	1953	The coronation of Queen Elizabeth II is watched by 20 million people on TV

WWII bomb damaged houses in Liverpool • *The war had caused the total destruction of 225,000 houses and the partial destruction of 550,000 more. For the next 30 years housing would be a government priority.*

Festival of Britain • *Experimental buildings at the Festival of Britain strongly influenced architecture and the rebuilding of Britain in the 1950s and 1960s.*
▼

A Tonic For the Nation

Looking forward to a brighter future, the government staged the Festival of Britain in the summer of 1951. The main site was the South Bank of the Thames at Lambeth in London. This was cleared of old Victorian buildings and railway **sidings** to be transformed into a thrilling exhibition of modern structures and inventions. More than 8.5 million visitors thronged to see the 100 metre tall Skylon, the vast aluminium Dome of Discovery and the starkly modern Festival Hall.

SOUNDBITES

Remember that $4 billion dollars Britain borrowed from America? That took a whopping 60 years to repay – with a final instalment of £45.5 million on 31st December 2006.

5

Population and Health Care

The British population has changed hugely since 1948 – there are far more people, they are healthier and they expect to live longer than ever before. In 1948, the population was about 47 million; by 2006 this had risen to about 60.2 million. The numbers will keep on growing to an estimated 61.5 million by 2011.

INVESTIGATE Population of the United Kingdom, June 2006

	Population	Percentage of total UK population
England	50,431,700	83.9%
Wales	2,958,600	4.9%
Scotland	5,094,800	8.5%
Northern Ireland	1,724,400	2.9%
United Kingdom	**60,209,500**	

Source: Office of National Statistics, June 2006

From 'the Cradle to the Grave'

One of the reasons the population has grown is better health care, which has cut the number of deaths. In 1945, a Labour government led by Clement Atlee was elected with the promise to set up a welfare state that would take care of people from 'the cradle to the grave.'

▲
***Creator of the NHS** • Aneurin Bevan visiting Papworth hospital in 1948.*

A key part of this was the National Health Service (NHS) set up in 1948. For the first time this offered free health care to all, including visits to the doctor, dentist and optician, together with any hospital treatment needed. Almost at once there was a flood of patients, with an estimated 6 million people alone needing glasses.

TIMELINE

1946	The first family allowances are paid, 25p for each child
1950	Richard Doll and Austin Bradford Hill publish their landmark study on the harmful effects of tobacco. This leads to a slow decline in the numbers of people smoking and dying of tobacco-related diseases
1955	The polio vaccine developed by Dr Jonas Salk. A huge vaccination programme begins in the UK and continues today
1968	The measles vaccine introduced. Before this around 0.5 million children caught measles and 100 died every year
2005/6	Spending on the NHS reaches £76 billion
2007	The smoking ban enforced in all public places in England from 1st July

Better health care soon had a positive impact on **infant mortality** and **life expectancy**. In 1948, 40 babies out of every thousand died before they were a year old. By 1978, this had fallen to about 12 per thousand and the figure is around five per thousand today. People are also living longer. In 1948, men lived to about 65 and women to 70 years old. By 1978, this had grown to 70 for men and 76 for women. Today the figure is 77 for men and 81 for women.

A Cleaner Environment Saves Lives

Working and living conditions also affected health. In 1948, Britain's cities were dirty places to live with fumes from coal burning fires, factory chimneys and motor vehicles polluting the air. In 1952, a winter smog, a poisonous mixture of smoke and fog, killed over 4,000 people in London. The government decided to introduce Clean Air Acts in 1956 and 1968 to cut air pollution such as smoke and fumes from homes and factories. Over the years these have saved the lives of many people with conditions like asthma and bronchitis.

Voices from history

'It is repugnant to a civilised community for hospitals to have to rely upon charity. I have always felt a shudder of repulsion when I have seen nurses and sisters who ought to be at their work, going about the streets collecting money for hospitals.'

In Place of Fear by Aneurin Bevan, the Secretary of State responsible for the formation of the NHS, 1952.

Dangerous air • People and a London bus struggle through the blinding smog of 1952. Thousands of tonnes of black soot, sticky particles of tar and gaseous sulphur dioxide were hanging in the air.

SOUNDBITES
Richard Dolls' pioneering study in 1950 of the dangers of smoking eventually led to the ban on public smoking in England on 1 July 2007.

The Changing World of Work

In 1948, 40% of the British workforce had jobs in **manufacturing**. Many of these jobs were in industries such as steel, coal and textiles, based in Scotland, Wales and Northern England. After a brief post war boom they saw a rapid decline. In 1945, for example, there were 50 steelworks in Ebbw Vale in South Wales; by 1970 there were seven. Today, there is only one large steel plant in Wales, at Port Talbot.

New Modes of Manufacturing

Despite problems, some new industries have thrived, such as chemicals (especially medicines), motor manufacturing and aero-engines. Even so by 2007, only 15% of the British workforce were employed in manufacturing.

TIMELINE

1956	The world's first nuclear power station, at Calder Hall in Cumbria, begins to generate power
1959	The launch of the British owned Austin Mini designed by Sir Alec Issigonis. The Mini was the first family car with front wheel drive and a hatchback instead of a boot
1984/5	A year-long miners' strike leads to the collapse of the mining industry
2001	The German company BMW relaunches the new Mini, built at Cowley in Oxford
2004	750,000 jobs in manufacturing lost since 1997

Voices from history

'My brother worked at the Rover plant in Longbridge, Birmingham and over 5,000 people lost their jobs there in 2005. It's not just the jobs though, it affects the whole community. Local services like shops have to close, and many people move away, making it harder for the people who have to stay.'

Tony, a steelworker interviewed on BBC Radio, 2007.

▲ **End of Rover** • The last large British-owned car maker, MG Rover closed in 2005 with a loss of 5,000 jobs. Britain is still a large car manufacturer, but the factories are owned by foreign companies like BMW (Germany) and Honda (Japan).

The cost of energy • A total of 167 people died when the Piper Alpha oil platform caught fire 120 miles off the north east coast of Scotland in 1988. Poor safety standards were to blame for the world's worst offshore oil disaster.

Rich Energy Resources

Britain has always been lucky in having rich energy resources. In 1948, the country still depended on coal for heating and electricity, but this was set to change. The Fortes Oilfield, the first in the North Sea, was discovered in 1969. Oil began to come ashore in 1975 when the Queen opened a new terminal at Grangemouth, near Aberdeen. British oil production hit a high of 3.1 million barrels a day in August 1999.

Moving South to Find Work

As manufacturing has declined over the last 60 years, more Britons than ever before work in services such as finance, retailing and leisure. Since the 1980s, many of these new jobs have been created in London and the south of England, and as you can see from the table on the right, this led to heavy **internal migration**. The census taken in 2001, showed that the fastest growing place over the previous 20 years had been Milton Keynes, with a population increase of 64%, while the population had fallen by 15% in Manchester.

INVESTIGATE — The UK's population changes between 1981 and 2001

	Population in 2001	Change
ENGLAND		
North East	2,515,479	- 4.60%
North West	6,729,800	- 3.00%
Yorks/Humber	4,964,838	- 0.90%
East Midlands	4,172,179	+ 8.00%
West Midlands	5,267,337	+ 1.60%
East of England	5,388,154	+ 11.00%
London	7,172,036	+ 5.40%
South East	8,000,550	+ 10.40%
South West	4,928,458	+ 12.50%
The nations		
SCOTLAND	5,062,011	- 2.00%
WALES	2,903,085	- 3.20%
N IRELAND	1,685,267	+ 9.00%

Source: Census 2001

▷ **Find the area you live in. Has the population risen or declined?**

The Baby Boomers

If one generation tells the story of Britain since 1948, it is the 'baby boomers'. This name means those born between 1945 and 1965 when there were 'booms' in the number of births compared to other decades, like the 1970s (see graph on page 11). The important thing about the baby boomers is that there are a lot of them – about 17 million. As they have grown up they have caused enormous changes to the way we live now.

1960s Teddy boys • *Teddy boys dressed in drainpipe trousers and often slicked back their hair.* ▶

TIMELINE

1945	The start of the 'Baby Boomer' years. These lasted from 1945–1965
1953	The first Teddy boys wear their drape coats
1964	1,014,700 births in the UK, the second highest total in the twentieth century
1965	Model Jean Shrimpton wears a shockingly short mini skirt, a symbol of 'the **permissive society'**
1968	Beatles LP *Sergeant Pepper's Lonely Hearts Club Band* storms the charts
1997	Baby Boomer Tony Blair becomes Prime Minister

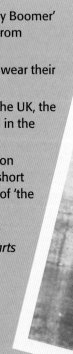

1960s youth cultures • Teddy boys and Hippies. Each of these groups had their own fashions and music. ▶

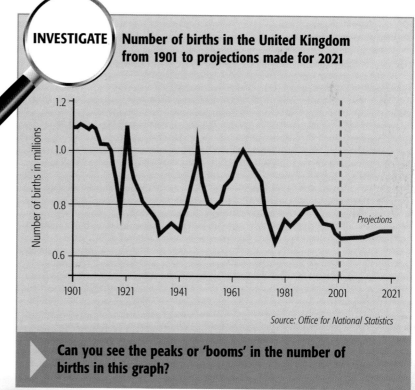

In the Beginning

The first baby boomers became teenagers in the 1950s and 1960s and started the idea that young people could have an identity different from their parents. Teddy boys were the original teen rebels. Rock n' roll fans, they dressed in Edwardian style jackets and drainpipe trousers. The 1960s, saw other youth groups, like hippies who wore colourful clothes with bells and beads, while skinheads were recognisable by their shaven heads.

Permissive Society

As they grew into young adults the baby boomers created what has been called 'the permissive society.' The **contraceptive** pill became available for the first time in 1960, and led to more relaxed ideas about sex before marriage. In the 1970s, women became more equal to men and went out to work in greater numbers. At the same time children were raised in families with fewer rules and less discipline.

Lucky and Greedy

The baby boomers have also been called the 'luckiest' and the 'greediest' generation. Compared to their parents, they enjoyed years of peace and high earnings. This lead to a **consumer culture**, with shopping as a major pastime for many people. In 1950, for example, there were 0.5 million fridges in British homes, but by 2007 this had soared to 37 million – more than a 60 fold increase. Now in their 50s and 60s, the first baby boomers control more than 80% of Britain's wealth.

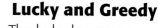

INVESTIGATE **Number of births in the United Kingdom from 1901 to projections made for 2021**

Number of births in millions

Projections

1901   1921   1941   1961   1981   2001   2021

Source: Office for National Statistics

▶ **Can you see the peaks or 'booms' in the number of births in this graph?**

The Changing Family

If you had been born in the late 1940s, what would your family have been like? You would probably have lived in a 'traditional' family, a term used by historians to mean a married couple living with their children. Your father would have married your mother when he was about 26–27 and she was around 23–24, perhaps one of the 307,000 couples that married in 1948.

The Traditional Family

Your mother was unlikely to have worked; only two out of ten married women did. Mothers were housewives and looked after their children.

The family would have lived on your father's wages – even if that meant doing without luxuries. Your parents would have married for life and if they became unhappy they would probably have put up with it. **Divorce** was still thought to be quite shocking and only about 20,000 marriages ended in divorce in 1948.

CHANGING TIMES

In 1971, only 8% of children were born to parents who were not married. In 2002, this figure had grown to 41%.

▲
The 1940s family • *This 1940s 'traditional' family gather round the radio for an evening of entertainment.*

TIMELINE

1948	307,000 couples marry but only 20,000 divorce
1961	One in three mothers now goes out to work
1969	The Divorce Reform Act
1972	480,000 couples marry, the peak year for marriages in the twentieth century
1993	180,000 couples divorce, the peak year for divorces in the twentieth century
1999	Only 301,000 couples get married, the lowest number in the twentieth century
2000	One in every three and a half marriages ends in divorce

Working Women

This stable family life was to change quite quickly. From 1955 to 1965, the economy boomed and employers looked to women to fill the new jobs. By 1961, one in three mothers went out to work and women made up almost half the workforce – more than during the Second World War. This became a growing trend, and by 2005, 70% of women worked, including seven out of ten mothers.

Divorce

Divorce has also shattered the traditional family picture. In 1961, there were 27,000 divorces, only a small rise from 1948. This had doubled to 56,000 by 1969 and it had doubled again to 125,000 by 1972. As a result of divorce becoming common, 25% of British children lived in one-parent families by 2005. In many cases a lone mother was the head of the family.

▲ **A common problem** • *The high rate of divorce today leaves many children feeling confused and upset. There are many support agencies who can offer advice, such as ChildLine.*

INVESTIGATE

In 1969, the Divorce Reform Act was passed, allowing couples to divorce after living apart for two years. What happened to the number of divorces after this change in the law?

Thousands

200

150

100

50

0

1961 1965 1969 1973 1977 1981 1985 1989 1983 1997 2001 2005

Source: Office of National Statistics

New Towns and Old Problems

By 1948, Britain had barely begun to repair the damage caused by German bombing. There was a terrible shortage of homes and thousands of desperate families took over empty houses, ex-army camps – and even old prisoner of war camps. New towns were a bold idea to improve living and working conditions.

New Towns Act

The Act of 1946 made plans for 11 new towns – eight around London, two in Scotland and one in County Durham. Planners borrowed ideas from the Victorian architect, Ebenezer Howard, who designed Welwyn Garden City, near London. Industry was to be separated from homes with lots of green, open spaces. Homes and shops were to be built from quality materials with new and exciting designs.

The UK • *This map shows some of the new towns that have developed since 1948.*

Cumbernauld

Irvine

Aycliffe

Telford

Milton Keynes

Stevenage

Basildon

Bracknell

Hatfield

Crawley

Welwyn Garden City

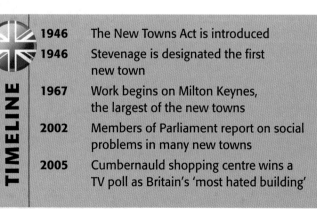

TIMELINE

1946	The New Towns Act is introduced	
1946	Stevenage is designated the first new town	
1967	Work begins on Milton Keynes, the largest of the new towns	
2002	Members of Parliament report on social problems in many new towns	
2005	Cumbernauld shopping centre wins a TV poll as Britain's 'most hated building'	

Successes and Failures

The first new towns were so successful that others soon followed including the expansion of Peterborough, Northampton and Warrington – a total of 33 since 1946. The largest is Milton Keynes in Buckinghamshire, which began in 1967. In 2006, the town proudly boasted a population of 215,000, 4,000 acres of parks and 20 million trees. Unemployment was at only 2% with 15,000 new jobs created between 2003 and 2006.

Other new towns have not been so lucky. A report by Members of Parliament (MPs) in 2002 said some were in danger of 'falling into a spiral of decline', with falling house prices and high crime rates. Problems included high unemployment and poorly built houses.

More New Towns

But the idea of new towns has not gone away. In 1993, Prince Charles started to build Poundbury, near Dorchester; a small town based on traditional materials and styles of architecture. In 2007, the government announced that five new environmentally friendly towns are to be built on **brown field** sites – the first at the abandoned Oakington barracks in Cambridgeshire. All their energy supplies will be found locally from sustainable sources, such as solar power.

An 'old' new town • Streets are deliberately narrow and winding to slow traffic down in Poundbury, near Dorchester.

Emigration: Brits go Abroad

Have your parents ever thought of living in another country? In the years between 1948 and 2005, more than 5 million British citizens did more than think about it – they emigrated. That means they left their homeland to live abroad. This was part of a long-term movement of people – for almost 400 years Britain has been a nation of emigrants.

Australia Calls

There were many reasons people chose to leave. Housing shortages in the 1940s and escape from unemployment and the hope of a better life in the 1950s and 1960s. More than 1 million people headed for Australia as 'ten pound poms'.

This was an 'assisted passage scheme' that cut the cost of the fare to just £10. For many **migrants** this meant a 12,000 mile voyage aboard a luxury liner like the *Canberra*.

INVESTIGATE **How to emigrate**
Most British emigrants went to countries that had once been part of the British Empire: Canada, Australia, New Zealand and South Africa.

▶ **How is the poster shown in the photograph designed to encourage British emigrants to come to Australia?**

TIMELINE

1947	The 'assisted passage scheme' to Australia begins, fares cost £10
1983	Britain becomes an importer of people with 17,000 more migrants coming in than emigrants going out. This trend continues for the next 20 years
2001	The Catholic Church in Australia apologises to child migrants from Britain who had been treated cruelly by Church agencies
2006	One in every ten Britons lives abroad, with Australia and Spain the favourite destinations

AUSTRALIA: ASSISTED PASSAGE APPLICATIONS

Australia welcomes you

A land of friendly birds See them soon.

▲

Australia welcomes you • In 1974 a gloomy economy led to a new rush of British emigrants to Australia. In Australia House in London people could apply to emigrate.

Many migrants built new lives in Australia, but for some the dream was quickly spoiled. They had to stay in temporary camps that had once been army bases. They had to put up with inspections and block leaders until they found jobs. Homesickness and disappointment led over a quarter to return home within two years.

Where to go? • *This map shows where most Britons lived in 2006.*

▼

The loud complaints of migrants led to the Australian nickname for the British – 'whinging poms'.

Child Migrants

Perhaps the saddest emigrants were unwanted children in the care of agencies like Barnados and the Fairbridge Society. More than 7,000 were sent to Australia between 1945 and 1967. Some, but not all, suffered abuse or cruelty at the hands of those trusted to look after them. The Catholic Church in Australia recognised and apologised for this cruelty in 2001.

CHANGING TIMES

Nearly 10% of Britons live abroad today, over 500,000 people. Another 58 million people worldwide claim British ancestry. Only the Chinese have spread around the world more than the British.

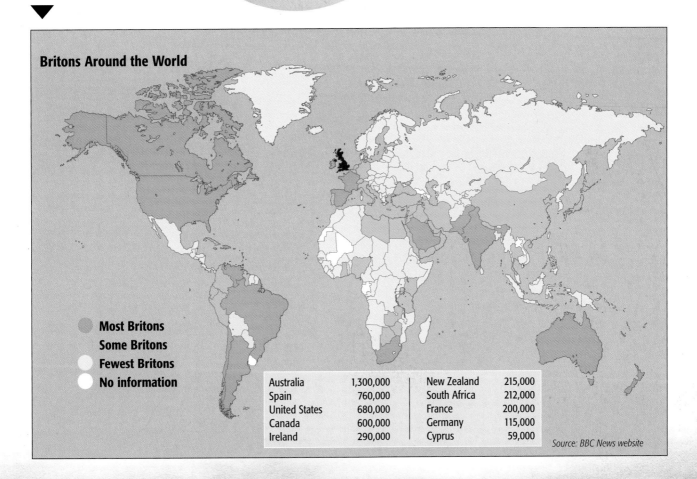

Britons Around the World

- ● Most Britons
- ● Some Britons
- ○ Fewest Britons
- ○ No information

Australia	1,300,000		New Zealand	215,000
Spain	760,000		South Africa	212,000
United States	680,000		France	200,000
Canada	600,000		Germany	115,000
Ireland	290,000		Cyprus	59,000

Source: BBC News website

Migration from Around the World

After the Second World War, Britain needed rebuilding, but there was a huge shortage of workers. To fill the empty jobs the government started an 'open door' policy for migrants from the **British Empire** and **Commonwealth**, inviting them to come and help 'the Motherland'. But how welcome would they be?

Come to the Motherland

Among the first were 492 Jamaicans who arrived aboard the *Empire Windrush* at Tilbury on 22 June 1948. This was a turning point in British history, the start of mass migration in modern times. Unfortunately many of those who arrived on the *Windrush* were to be upset by the prejudice they faced in Britain. By 1961, about 180,000 people from the West Indies had settled in the UK, most of them finding jobs in transport and the building trades. In the 1950s and 1960s, textile and engineering firms in the north of England advertised for workers in India and Pakistan.

This kick started the migration from South Asia, which continued through the 1970s and 1980s, as wives and children joined their husbands and fathers. By 2001, there were more than a million Indians and 747,000 Pakistanis in the UK, with more than half of them born here. With them came a religious diversity never seen in Britain before. The Indians were mainly Hindus and Sikhs, while the Pakistanis were almost all Muslims.

Emergency Migrants

Britain has a long history of offering safety to **refugees** escaping wars or cruel governments. In the 1940s and 1950s, Poles and Hungarians fled **communist** states in Eastern Europe and were soon followed by many others. Between 1968 and 1972, 50,000 Asians living in East Africa arrived in Britain after they were expelled from Kenya and Uganda by **dictators** such as Idi Amin.

TIMELINE

1948	The British Nationality Act gives every Commonwealth citizen the right of entry to Britain
2001	A census shows that the ethnic minority population has grown from 3 million to 4.6 million people since 1991, an increase of 50%
1993–2002	One million more people come to live in the UK than leave to live in other countries

CHANGING TIMES

Most of the migrants on the *Empire Windrush* in 1948 were ex-servicemen who had fought for the British Empire in the Second World War. They expected a better welcome than many received.

The first of many • *Caribbean migrants arrive aboard the* Empire Windrush, *a turning point in the history of migration into Britain.*

The 1980s, saw thousands of Vietnamese 'boat people' arrive, so called because of the desperate escapes they made across the South China Sea in small, overcrowded boats. In the 1990s, Somalis fled civil war and starvation in the Horn of Africa, often walking hundreds of miles to safety in refugee camps in Ethiopia and Kenya. By about 2005, around 30,000 Vietnamese and 70,000 Somalis had sought refuge in the UK.

INVESTIGATE | **The non-white population of Great Britain, 1951–2001**

Year	Non-white population
1951	30,000 (est)
1961	400,000 (est)
1971	1.4 million
1981	2.1 million
1991	3.0 million
2001	4.6 million

Source: Commission for Racial Equality Fact File 2, 2007

▶ **Which decade saw the greatest growth in the non-white population of Britain?**

Multicultural Britain: Problems and Achievements

Black and Asian immigrants arriving after 1948 faced prejudice from the white population. They were turned away from lodgings by signs saying 'No Blacks' or were banned from local pubs and cafes. As migrant numbers grew so did the tensions between races, at worst turning into violence. In 1958, there were riots in the Notting Hill area of London when white gangs attacked West Indians. Trouble flared during most nights throughout August and early September as mobs broke shop windows and fought with police.

Race riots • *There were race riots across many inner cities in Britain in 1981 when black communities protested against ill treatment by the police.*

TIMELINE

1958	Race riots in Notting Hill, London
1962	The Commonwealth Immigration Act tightens entry controls so that Commonwealth citizens need a work permit
1985	Police Constable Keith Blakelock stabbed to death on the North London estate, Broadwater Farm
1987	Four non-white Members of Parliament are elected to Parliament
2001	Problems of **racism**, poverty and unemployment spark riots in Bradford, Burnley and Oldham

Race Riots

In April 1981, Brixton in South London became a battlefield as black youths rebelled against police 'sus' laws. These laws gave the police the power to stop and search suspects. By July, many other districts up and down the entire country, including Mosley in Birmingham and Toxteth in Liverpool, had seen similar protests.

Voices from history

'Things are changing very much and people aren't as prejudiced as they used to be towards coloured people. When I first came here it was, 'Wogs go home' and all sort of graffiti written on the side of houses and all sorts of things. They must have thought we're not human. That's how I see it. To me they thought we're not human.'

Joyce Watson interviewed by Channel 4, in 2006. Joyce was born in 1935 and emigrated from Jamaica to Bradford in 1962, when she was 26 years old.

New Laws

The government responded in two ways to improve race relations. The first was to tighten immigration controls so that by 1971 Commonwealth citizens had no more rights to enter Britain than people from any other country. The second was to use the law to make many kinds of discrimination illegal. The Race Relations Act of 1976 gave people who felt they had not been treated equally the right to go to an employment tribunal or the courts.

Black heroes • Athlete Kelly Holmes won two gold medals for the 800 and 1,500 metre races at the Athens Olympic Games in 2004. Other ethnic minority sporting heroes include Formula One racing driver Lewis Hamilton and boxer Amir Khan. ▶

A tragic event forced Britain to look closely at the dangers of prejudice again in 1993 – the murder of an 18-year-old A-level student, Stephen Lawrence by a white gang. The repeated failure of the police to investigate his killing properly led his parents to fight a long campaign for a government report. In 1999, the Lawrence Inquiry found that the police had been incompetent and racist. This led to huge improvements in police training and the investigation of race crimes.

In spite of the problems many faced, Britain's **ethnic minorities** have brought a rich variety to every day life over the past 60 years. A takeaway meal in 1948 would have been fish and chips, now it might be Chinese, Italian or Turkish. Music styles from Jamaican Calypso and Reggae, to Indian classical and Bhangra attract large audiences. In 1993, Paul Ince became the first black football player to captain England, while Nasser Hussein achieved the same honour for cricket in 1999.

Migration from Europe

Since ancient times Britain has absorbed waves of migrants from Europe but since 1945 the numbers moving here have soared. The story of the Poles is one of the most fascinating. As with Commonwealth citizens, Britain invited Poles to help rebuild the country after the Second World War – and many were desperate to take up the offer. Thousands of Polish servicemen who had fought for Britain had no country to go back to – Poland had become a communist state. By 1951, over 160,000 Polish refugees had settled in Britain.

Under Communist Control

Poland was part of Eastern Europe controlled by the **Soviet Union** and few people were allowed to leave. Even letters and phone calls to relatives in Britain were checked by the secret police.

Finally in 1989, peaceful revolutions led to the collapse of communist governments in Poland, East Germany, Czechoslovakia, Hungary and Bulgaria. People were free to travel once again.

Gallant allies • *This photograph shows two polish pilots who fought in the RAF during the Second World War against Nazi Germany even when their own country had been conquered.* ▼

TIMELINE

1940	Polish pilots fight in the Battle of Britain
1945	A communist government is set up in Poland under the control of the Soviet Union (Russia)
1973	Britain joins the **European Union**
1987	The Single European Act allows free movement of 'goods, persons and services' throughout the EU
2004	Poland joins the EU and many young Poles head for Britain

Settling down • *Large numbers of Polish businesses are being set up in Britain to serve the needs of the new migrants.*

EU Citizens

In 2004, Poland was one of 10 new countries that joined the European Union – and gained the right for its citizens to work anywhere in the EU, including Britain. The British government expected around 13,000 Poles to come and look for jobs, but it was in for a shock. Britain was about to experience the biggest influx of people ever. By 2006, more than 600,000 Eastern Europeans had arrived and more than half of them Poles.

SOUNDBITES
Some towns are changing very quickly. In Crewe more than 6% of the population were Polish by 2006.

CHANGING TIMES

David Coleman, Professor of Population Studies at Oxford University, has compared the impact of Poles arriving in the UK to the arrival of the **Huguenots** from France in the seventeenth century. In both cases large numbers of a single national group moved to Britain in a short space of time.

Many were skilled workers and quickly found jobs in building, farming, restaurants, shopping and health care. In July 2007, an opinion poll published in Poland by the newspaper *Gazeta Wyborcza*, said 55% of Poles who work in Britain plan to stay for at least 10 years.

Rising Crime

People who remember life in 1948 often say they could go out without locking their doors and no-one would steal from them, just like it says in Frederick's poem (opposite). Certainly the number of reported crimes in England and Wales was much lower than today, at 522,000 in 1948. As for the worst crimes, there were only 341 murders in England and Wales and another 34 in Scotland.

Crime Soars

Crime levels stayed about the same until 1959, when offences began to climb steeply, reaching a record high of more than 6 million crimes in England and Wales in 2003–2004. The worst year for murders in England and Wales was 2002–2003 with 1,047 killings, while the worst year in Scotland was 2004–2005 with 137 killings.

TIMELINE

1955	The last woman is hanged in the UK (Ruth Ellis at Holloway Prison)
1964	Peter Anthony Allen and Gwynne Owen Evans are the last men hanged. Their executions take place at the same time
1972	Community Service Orders are introduced as an alternative punishment to fines and jail
1995	Electronic tagging is piloted in Manchester for the first time
2002	Community Service now called Community Punishment

Voices from history

'Times were hard and that's a fact
But one thing was for sure
Folks were kind and honest
No need to lock your door.
Nothing much was ever pinched
No need to count the cost
To pinch owt good from our house
They got to bring the bloomin
thing fost.'

Let's Walk Down Memory Lane, Frederick Alletson remembering the 1940s in this poem he wrote in 2004 on the BBC People's War website.

▲ **Dramatic changes** • *The image of the police has changed dramatically, from the friendly image of TV's Dixon of Dock Green in this photograph.*

Reasons for Rising Crime

So why has crime got so much worse? Well there's a clue in Frederick's poem. Since the 1940s, Britain has become much richer and there is far more to steal. Take car crime for example: just 2 million people owned cars in 1948; now there are over 30 million on the roads. As a result car crime has soared, with 1.7 million incidents of vehicle crime reported in 2005–2006. Changes in technology, too, have led to new crimes, such as computer hacking and internet fraud.

Cruel Punishment Abolished

The last 60 years have seen important changes in the way offenders are treated. **Flogging** was abolished in 1948. The last executions for murder took place in 1964, and the death penalty was abolished in 1969, after unease that innocent people were hanged for murders they did not commit.

Prison and Community Service

Around 20,000 people were sent to prison in England and Wales in 1948, this grew to a record 81,000 by 2006. An alternative to prison, the Community Service Order, was introduced in 1972. Criminals could be ordered to attend meetings with **probation officers** or do unpaid work.

By the 1990s, Community Service had become the most widely used punishment but had not stopped the rise in offenders sent to prison. In 1995, electronic tagging was introduced in Manchester to keep tabs on those who had received a Community Service Order as a punishment.

SOUNDBITES
The number of police officers has grown from around 60,000 in the 1940s, to a record high of 141,000 in 2005. The public always want to see more police officers on the beat. The number of police officers has risen as the population increased.

▲

Police today • The image of the police has changed dramatically over the decades, from the friendly image of PC Dixon to a force that has to tackle street riots and terrorism as well as ordinary crimes.

A Fighting Nation

During the Second World War, British armed services were at their biggest ever. There were almost 2.9 million men and women in the army, 1.1 million in the RAF and 900,000 in the Royal Navy. Numbers were cut rapidly when the war ended in 1945, but even so in 1948, the armed forces were still 830,000 strong.

A Nation in Arms

In the years after the war Britain remained a great power while slowly giving up a huge empire. In 1948, the UK joined **NATO** to face down the Soviet Union in the **Cold War**. This meant keeping a large **garrison** in Germany in case of a Russian invasion. At the same time troops fought small wars in places as far flung as Malaya from 1948–1960, Korea from 1950–1953 and Suez in 1956.

National Service

To find enough men to fight, the government brought in peacetime National Service, compelling most young men to go into the army, Navy or RAF for two years. National Service lasted from 1945–1963 and during that time 2.5 million men joined up – 6,000 every fortnight. Discipline was tough and new recruits who annoyed their drill sergeant could be ordered to run around the **barrack square** while wearing a gas mask – or even scrub the parade ground with a toothbrush. Each year some National Servicemen saw action and a total of 395 National Servicemen were killed.

CHANGING TIMES

Women made up around 9% of service personnel in 2005.

About 3,500 Gurkhas from Nepal served in the army in 2006, together with around 1,800 Fijians.

Endless drills • *Training for National Servicemen was tough with endless drilling in squads and learning to react instantly to orders.*

TIMELINE

1948	Peacetime conscription is introduced
1963	The launch of HMS *Dreadnought*, the Royal Navy's first nuclear powered submarine
1982	Falklands War against Argentina
2003	Invasion of Iraq

Nuclear Weapons

From the 1960s onwards, Britain relied on smaller armed forces backed by more nuclear weapons. At first these were free fall bombs carried by RAF Vulcan bombers, but in the 1970s, the Royal Navy took over with nuclear submarines carrying Polaris **ballistic missiles**. Some historians argue that this **nuclear deterrent** stopped the Cold War becoming a deadly hot war because both sides were scared of wiping each other out.

Trouble in the Atlantic

In 1982, Britain sent a powerful naval task force 8,000 miles to the South Atlantic to recapture the Falkland Islands from Argentina. Remarkably, just seven weeks after the Argentines invaded, British troops began landing at San Carlos Bay and fought their way across East Falkland to liberate the tiny capital, Stanley. In 2007, British armed forces

A long campaign • *The British army fought the Irish Republican Army from 1968–2005. The IRA wanted to unite Northern and Southern Ireland. The British army didn't defeat the IRA but did help bring lasting peace.*

were at their smallest since 1945, just under 180,000. Troops were in action in Iraq and Afghanistan fighting Muslim terrorists in controversial wars that bitterly divided public opinion.

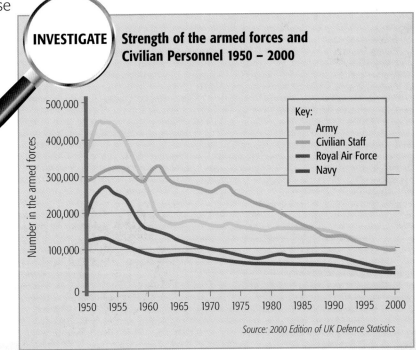

INVESTIGATE · **Strength of the armed forces and Civilian Personnel 1950 – 2000**

Number in the armed forces

500,000
400,000
300,000
200,000
100,000
0

1950 1955 1960 1965 1970 1975 1980 1985 1990 1995 2000

Key:
Army
Civilian Staff
Royal Air Force
Navy

Source: 2000 Edition of UK Defence Statistics

Living on a Crowded Island

If you compare your local area with maps from around 1948, you will see how the towns have sprawled out into the countryside. With a rising population the UK has become one of the most heavily populated countries in the world. In 2003, there were 383 people per square kilometre in England, but just 106 in France and two in Australia.

Protected by the Green Belt

The dangers of uncontrolled building destroying the countryside were spotted in the 1930s, but it was not until 1947 that the government introduced the Town and Country Planning Act. The Act allowed councils to set up green belts – protected areas of countryside to stop towns growing so much that they merged into each other. This has helped keep the character of UK communities and provided leisure and recreation for their people.

Conservation success • *The green belt gives town and city dwellers green space to escape into and preserves some of the best landscapes in Britain.*

Voices from history

'When I was a lad in the early 1950s we could walk out of Sunderland, past the allotments into the countryside. It was less than a mile. From Tunstall Hill we could see right over the town – and there were fields all round. Now most of them have been built on. It's hard to get a sense of space today.'

Maurice Vleugals, interviewed in 2007.

TIMELINE

1949	London's first ten-storey council housing block is opened in Holborn
1980	People renting council houses are given the right to buy them
1999	Bluewater, Europe's largest retail and leisure centre is opened in Kent on 16 March
2003	More than 1.5 million people have bought their council houses since 1980, leading to a national shortage of homes to rent
2007	The Office for National Statistics estimates the population will increase to 65 million by 2016

Green belts now cover 13% of England. Even so many towns and cities have changed alot since the 1940s. Huge council estates and rows of tower blocks were built in the 1950s and 1960s when Labour and Conservative governments raced one another to construct the most new homes. In 1968, a record was set when 417,000 new dwellings were built.

Out of Town

Since the 1970s, 'out-of-town' developments for living, working and shopping have boomed. The first company Laser-Scan moved into the hi-tec Cambridge Science Park in 1973. In 1985, work started on the first big retail park, the Metro Centre near Gateshead.

Housing Shortages

In the twenty first century the UK faces severe shortages of housing to meet the needs of a rising population. The government wants to match this demand by building up to a million new homes, many in the Thames Gateway.

Go-ahead Gateway • *There are plans to build 160,000 homes in the Thames Gateway. This project will create 180,000 jobs by 2016.*

▼

INVESTIGATE | **UK Population Density**

	People per Square Kilometre
England	383
Scotland	65
Wales	142
Northern Ireland	125

Source: National Statistics Online, 2005

This will be the largest regeneration project in Western Europe. It will stretch 60 kilometres from East London on both sides of the River Thames and the Thames Estuary, to Southend-on-Sea and the Isle of Sheppey. The project will not only create new homes. It will also generate employment for those in the area.

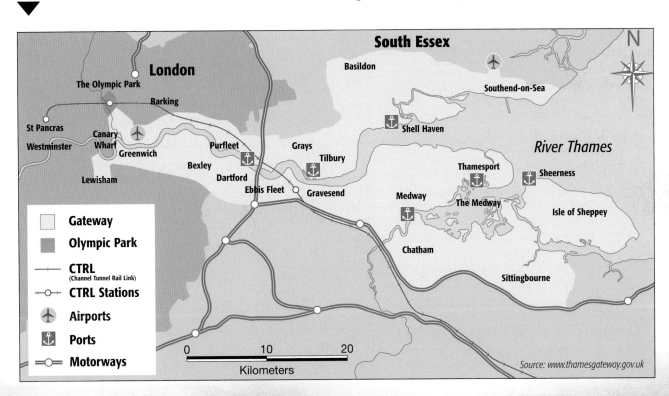

Timeline *Highlights in the History of Britain since 1948*

1948 British Nationality Act gives every Commonwealth citizen the right of entry to Britain

1948 160,000 emergency houses called prefabs built

1948 307,000 couples marry but only 20,000 get divorced

1949 London's first ten-storey council housing block opened in Holborn

1951 Festival of Britain

1953 Coronation of Queen Elizabeth II

1955 Polio vaccine developed by Dr Jonas Salk

1958 Race riots in Notting Hill, London

1960 1,01,014,700 births in the UK

1961 One in three mothers goes out to work

1962 Commonwealth Immigration Act tightens entry controls so that Commonwealth citizens need a work permit

1967 Work begins on Milton Keynes, the largest of the new towns

1968 Measles vaccine introduced

1969 Divorce Reform Act introduced. Couples can divorce after living apart for two years

1972 480,000 couples married

1973 Britain joins the European Union

1980 People renting council houses are given the right to buy them

1982 Falklands War against Argentina

1987 Single European Act allows free movement of 'goods, persons and services' throughout the EU

1993 180,000 couples divorce

1993-2002 1 million more people come to live in the UK than leave to live in other countries

1999 Only 301,000 couples marry, the lowest number in the twentieth century

2000 One in every three and a half marriages ends in divorce

2001 The Catholic Church in Australia apologises to child migrants from Britain who had been treated cruelly by Church agencies

2002 MP's report on social problems in many new towns

2003 More than 1.5 million people have bought their council houses since 1980, leading to a national shortage of council housing

2003 Invasion of Iraq

2004 Poland joins the EU and many young Poles head for Britain

2005/6 Spending on the NHS reaches £76 billion

2006 One in every 10 Britons lives abroad, with Australia and Spain as the favourite destinations

Glossary

ballistic missile A missile that is guided but eventually falls under gravity on its target

barrack square A drill ground

brown field Land that has already been used

British Empire The regions of the world that were once ruled by Britain, which reached its height in power in the 1920s and 1930s

Cold War A war between Soviet countries and America

Commonwealth Association of countries once in the British Empire

communist Dictatorship that is supposed to give workers control of their country

consumer culture People buying far more than they need

contraceptive A means of stopping a woman becoming pregnant

dictators Rulers who govern with total power over a country

divorce Legally ending a marriage

ethnic minority Belonging to an ethnic group which is not the main ethnicity of the population

European Union The countries of Europe that belong to the Union

flogging Beating

garrison A body of troops stationed in a town to defend it

Huguenots French Protestants who came to Britain in the seventeenth century

infant mortality The death of children under the age of one year

internal migration People moving from one place to another within their own country

life expectancy How long people can expect to live

manufacturing Producing things

migrants People who move from place to place

NATO North Atlantic Treaty Organisation, an alliance between America, Canada and Western Europe

nuclear deterrent A nuclear weapon that countries will not use against each other for fear of wiping each other out

permissive society Relaxed attitudes about how people dress and behave compared to past generations

probation officers A person who supervises offenders on probation

racism Unfair treatment because of race

refugee A person who has been forced to leave their country because of war, danger or natural disaster

sidings Areas where railway locomotives and carriages are parked

Soviet Union Federation of communist countries led by Russia

FURTHER INFORMATION

📖 Books

Britain Since World War II: Health and Diet
Stewart Ross
(Franklin Watts, 2007)

The Geography Detective Investigates: Your Local Area
Ruth Jenkins
(Wayland, 2006)

Explore History: Britain Since 1930
Jane Shuter
(Heinemann Library, 2005)

🖱 Websites

http://www.museumoflondon.org.uk/archive/exhibits/festival/
Look back to the spectacular Festival of Britain

http://www.metoffice.gov.uk/education/secondary/students/smog.html
Would you have survived the great Smog?

http://www.statistics.gov.uk/census/2011Census/default.asp
Check out the plans for the 2011 census – it's important and you'll be in it.

http://www.movinghere.org.uk/
You can research 200 years of migration in England

Index

Numbers in **bold** type refer to an illustration.

BRITAIN SINCE 1948

Contents of titles in the series:

WAYLAND